Vegetarian Cookbook

The best beginner's guide,
delicious recipes for kids
Vol.2

Matt Alemu

Table of Contents

1. Christmas to find. Rainbow fruit skewers

7 raspberries• 7 hulled strawberries• 7 tangerine segments• 7 cubes peeled mango• 7 peeled pineapple chunks• 7 peeled kiwi fruit chunks• 7 green grapes• 7 red grapes• 14 blueberries

DIRECTIONS (15 minutes)

1 Take 7 wooden skewers and thread the following fruit onto each – 1 raspberry, 1 hulled strawberry,1 tangerine segment, 1 cube of peeled mango, 1 chunk of peeled pineapple, 1 chunk of peeled kiwi,1 green and 1 red grape, and finish off with 2 blueberries. Arrange in a rainbow shape and let everyone help themselves.

Notes:

2. Baked camembert kit

INGREDIENTS (2 Servings)

100g sultana• 5 tbsp Calvados , PX Sherry, rum or brandy• 1 boxed camembert To complete the kit• small jar , string or ribbon and a label

DIRECTIONS (20 minutes)

1 Heat sultanas and alcohol together until just simmering, then turn off the heat and cool completely. Spoon into a small jar and seal. Put the jar on top of the cheese and tie together with string or ribbon. 2 Keep in the fridge for up to a week until you are ready to give them away, then add a label with these instructions: 'Heat oven to 200C/fan 180C/gas 6. Unwrap the camembert, take off the wax wrapper and any other packaging. Put it back in the box but leave the lid off. Cook for 10 mins or until the centre of the cheese feels very soft. Cut a slashed cross in the centre of the cheese then tip in and over as many of the sultanas as you like. Serve with chunks of crusty bread.'

Notes:

3. Puff pastry pizzas

320g sheet ready-rolled light puff pastry• 6 tbsp tomato purée• 1 tbsp tomato ketchup• 1 tsp dried oregano• 75g mozzarella or cheddar For the topping • sweetcorn , olives, peppers, red onion, cherry tomatoes, spinach, basil

DIRECTIONS (45 minutes)

1 Heat the oven to 200C/180C fan/gas 6. Unroll the pastry, cut into six squares and arrange over two baking trays lined with baking parchment. Use a cutlery knife to score a 1cm border around the edge of each pastry square. Bake for 15 mins, until puffed up but not cooked through. 2 While the pastry cooks, make the sauce and prepare your toppings. Mix the tomato purée, tomato ketchup, oregano and 1 tbsp water. Grate the cheese and chop any veg or herbs you want to put on top into small pieces. Set aside. 3 Remove the pastry from the oven and squash down the middles with the back of a spoon. Divide the sauce between the pastry squares and spread it out to the puffed-up edges. Sprinkle with the cheese, then add your toppings. Bake for another 5-8 mins and serve.

Notes:

4. Chewy cranberry choc-nut cookie kit

1 large (1 litre approx) jar - Kilner or with a good screw lid• 100g caster sugar• 100g light muscovado sugar• 250g self-raising flour• 85g macadamia nut , roughly chopped• 85g dried cranberry• 100g white chocolate chip , buttons, or roughly chopped chunks

DIRECTIONS (30 minutes)

1 Clean the jar and dry well. Layer in the ingredients, starting with the caster sugar, followed by the muscovado, flour, nuts, cranberries and finally finishing with the white chocolate. Close the jar, then add a label with baking instructions, plus a ribbon or pretty cover if you like.

Notes:

5. Gravadlax kit

• 1 orange• 1 dill plant• small pot of black peppercorns• 125g box of sea salt• 500g bag of demerara sugar• small pot of coriander seeds• small pot of caraway seeds• a fishmonger gift voucher (to buy a 500g boneless piece of salmon)• pestle and mortar (optional)

DIRECTIONS (55 minutes)

1 To use the kit: Write the following instructions on the gift tag:To make the cure for your gravadlax, zest the orange and roughly chop a large bunch of dill. Using a pestle and mortar, grind 1 /2 tbsp peppercorns, then stir in 50g sea salt, 75g sugar, 1 tsp each coriander seeds and caraway seeds, and the zest. 2 Put half the dill on a large piece of cling film and place your salmon on top. Cover with all the cure and the remaining dill, then wrap tightly. Place in a dish with something heavy on top to weigh it down. 3Leave to cure for 24-48 hrs, turning the salmon once, then rinse well and pat dry before serving. Will keep in the fridge for up to three days.

Notes:

6. Satay chicken & mango wraps

INGREDIENTS (4 Servings)

5 tbsp smooth peanut butter• 160ml can coconut cream• 1 tbsp soy sauce• 2 tbsp mango chutney• zest 1 lime , plus wedges to serve• 4 skinless chicken breasts , cut into chunky pieces• 300g pack chopped mango• 2 carrots , grated or julienned• handful coriander leaves (optional)• 4 wraps , warmed

DIRECTIONS (30 minutes)

1 In a large bowl, mix the peanut butter, coconut cream, soy, mango chutney and lime zest. Spoon half into a serving bowl and set aside. Add the chicken pieces to the large bowl and toss everything well to coat. Can be left to marinate in the fridge for up to 24 hrs. 2 Thread the chicken onto skewers (you should make 4-6), alternating the chunks with pieces of mango. Place on a baking tray lined with foil. Heat the grill to high and cook the skewers for 5 mins each side until the chicken is cooked through and starting to char on the edges. Serve in warm wraps with bowls of carrot, coriander, extra satay sauce and lime wedges for squeezing over.

Notes:

7. Chocolate fudge Easter cakes

Chocolate fudge easter cakes • 140g soft butter• 140g golden caster sugar• 3 medium eggs• 100g self-raising flour• 25g cocoa , sifted For the frosting • 85g milk chocolate , broken• 85g soft butter• 140g icing sugar , sifted• 235g/1.5oz packs white chocolate maltesers, mini foil-wrapped chocolate eggs We use Fairtrade Divine milk chocolate eggs from Waitrose

DIRECTIONS (15 minutes)

1 Heat oven to 190C/fan 170C/gas 5 and put 16 gold cases into a fairy-cake tin. Tip all the ingredients for the cake into a mixing bowl and beat for 2 mins with an electric hand-whisk until smooth. Divide between the cases so they are two-thirds filled, then bake for 12-15 mins until risen. Cool on a wire rack. 2 For the frosting, microwave the chocolate on High for 1 min. Cream the butter and sugar together, then beat in the melted chocolate. Spread on the cakes and decorate with Maltesers and chocolate eggs.

Notes:

8. Easter egg rocky road

INGREDIENTS (5 Servings)

225g dark chocolate , broken into pieces• 100g unsalted butter , cubed• 2 tbsp cocoa powder• 2 tbsp golden syrup• 100g rich tea biscuits• 50g mini marshmallows• 50g dried cranberries• 200g chocolate mini eggs

DIRECTIONS (1 hour 25 minutes)

1 Line a 20 x 30cm traybake tin with 2 sheets of cling film (in a criss-cross pattern). Put the chocolate and butter in a large bowl set over a saucepan of gently simmering water, and melt until smooth and glossy. 2Remove from the heat and add the cocoa powder and golden syrup. Mix together until fully combined and leave to cool at room temperature for about 15 mins. 3 Put the biscuits in a freezer bag and use a rolling pin to bash them, leaving some pieces chunkier than others. Stir into the cooled chocolate with the marshmallows, cranberries and 150g of the mini eggs. 4 Pour the mix into the tin and press down with the back of a spoon until even. Scatter over the remaining mini eggs, pressing them in a little, and leave to set in the fridge for 1 hr. 5Remove from the tin and cut into bars to serve. Will keep for up to 1 week in an airtight container.

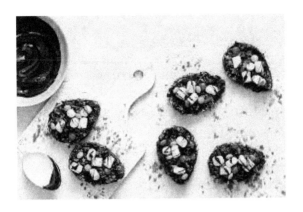

Notes:

9. Family meals: Mild chicken curry

• 1-1½ tsp coconut oil (we used Fushi) or sunflower oil• 1 large onion, finely chopped• 2 fat garlic cloves, crushed• 1cm fresh ginger, grated or finely chopped• 1 tsp ground coriander• 1 tsp yellow mustard seed• 1 tsp garam masala• ½ tsp ground cumin• 1 x 500g pack chicken pieces (thighs and drumsticks), or thighs• 1 chicken stock cube• 1 cinnamon stick• 250g Greek yogurt, at room temperature• 2 tbsp sultana• handful chopped coriander, to serve (optional)

DIRECTIONS (1 hour 30 minutes)

1 Heat the oil in a heavy-based pan. Fry the onions gently for 5 – 10 mins until soft. Add the garlic, ginger, coriander, mustard seeds, garam masala and cumin and cook for 1 - 2 min allowing the aromas to release. 2 Add the chicken and cook for 10 mins over a gentle heat, flipping occasionally and making sure the spices don't catch. Pour in around 300 ml boiling water until almost covering. Stir in the stock cube and cinnamon stick. Simmer for around 45 mins - 1 hour with the lid off so there is a small amount of thickened sauce at the bottom of the pan. Remove the cinnamon stick. 3Stir in the yogurt and sultanas, heat through gently and serve. Scatter with coriander, if using.

Notes:

10. Simple nutty pancakes

• 150g self-raising flour• ½ tsp baking powder• 1 large egg•
150ml milk• 2 tbsp agave syrup , plus extra to serve• 50g mixed
nuts , chopped• 2 tbsp rapeseed oil , for frying

DIRECTIONS (10 minutes)

1 Tip the flour and baking powder into a large bowl with a pinch
of salt. Make a well in the centre, then add the egg, milk and syrup.
Whisk until smooth, then fold in half the nuts. 2 Heat 1 tbsp oil in
a large, non-stick frying pan over a medium-high heat. Spoon two
ladles of the mixture into the pan and cook for 1 min each side.
Repeat to make two more. 3Serve with a drizzle of agave syrup
and the remaining nuts for extra crunch.

Notes:

11. Flowerpot chocolate chip muffins

INGREDIENTS (10 Servings)

• 3 tbsp vegetable oil• 125g plain flour• 1 tsp baking powder• 25g cocoa powder• 100g golden caster sugar• 1 large egg• 100ml milk• 150g milk chocolate chips• 25g chocolate cake decorations such as vermicelli sprinkles or chocolate-coated popping candy • 20 rice paper wafer daisies (these come in packs of 12, so get 2 packs) You will need• 10 mini teracotta pots (see tip)

DIRECTIONS (37 minutes)

1Heat oven to 180C/160C fan/gas 4. Lightly oil the inside of the terracotta pots with a little vegetable oil and place on a baking tray. Place a paper mini muffin case in the bottom of each pot. 2Put the flour, baking powder and cocoa in a bowl and stir in the sugar. 3 Crack the egg into a jug and whisk with the milk and remaining oil. Pour this over the flour and cocoa mixture, and stir in with 50g of the chocolate chips. Be careful not to overmix – you want a loose but still quite lumpy mixture. Spoon into the pots up to three-quarters full. Place in the middle of the oven and bake for 12-15 mins until risen and firm. Transfer to a wire rack (still in the pots) and leave to cool. 4 Put the rest of the chocolate chips in a small bowl and melt over a small pan of gently simmering water (don't let the water touch the bowl), or put in a microwave-proof bowl and heat on High for 1 min until melted. 5 Spread the tops of the muffins with the melted chocolate. Sprinkle over the chocolate decorations and add 2 rice paper wafer daisies to each pot to serve. Will keep for 2 days in an airtight container.

Notes:

12. Sticky plum flapjack bars

• 450g fresh plum , halved, stoned and roughly sliced• ½ tsp mixed spice• 300g light muscovado sugar• 350g butter , plus extra for greasing• 300g rolled porridge oats (not jumbo)• 140g plain flour• 50g chopped walnut pieces• 3 tbsp golden syrup

DIRECTIONS (1 hour 20 minutes)

1Heat oven to 200C/180C fan/gas 6. Tip the plums into a bowl. Toss with the spice, 50g of the sugar and a small pinch of salt, then set aside to macerate. 2 Gently melt the butter in a saucepan. In a large bowl, mix the oats, flour, walnut pieces and remaining sugar together, making sure there are no lumps of sugar, then stir in the butter and golden syrup until everything is combined into a loose flapjack mixture. 3 Grease a square baking tin about 20 x 20cm. Press half the oaty mix over the base of the tin, then tip over the plums and spread to make an even layer. Press the remaining oats over the plums so they are completely covered right to the sides of the tin. Bake for 45-50 mins until dark golden and starting to crisp a little around the edges. Leave to cool completely, then cut into 18 little bars. Will keep in an airtight container for 2 days or can be frozen for up to a month.

Notes:

13. Easter chocolate bark

• 3 x 200g bars milk chocolate• 2 x 90g packs mini chocolate eggs• 1 heaped tsp freeze-dried raspberry pieces – or you could use crystallised petals

1 Break the chocolate into a large heatproof bowl. Bring a pan of water to a simmer, then sit the bowl on top. The water must not touch the bottom of the bowl. Let the chocolate slowly melt, stirring now and again with a spatula. For best results, temper your chocolate (see tip). 2 Meanwhile, lightly grease then line a 23 x 33cm roasting tin or baking tray with parchment. Put three-quarters of the mini eggs into a food bag and bash them with a rolling pin until broken up a little. 3 When the chocolate is smooth, pour it into the tin. Tip the tin from side to side to let the chocolate find the corners and level out. Scatter with the smashed and whole mini eggs, followed by the freeze-dried raspberry pieces. Leave to set, then remove from the parchment and snap into shards, ready to pack in boxes or bags.

Notes:

14. Really easy roast chicken

• 1 whole chicken , about 1.5kg• 1 lemon , halved• 2 garlic cloves•
thyme or rosemary sprig, if you have it• 50g soft butter• 800g
very small salad potato , such as Charlotte, halved if you can
only find large ones • 350g small Chantenay carrot , or 3-4
regular carrots. cut into chunks• 1 tbsp olive oil• 300ml chicken
stock• 1 tbsp low-salt soy sauce

1 KIDS: The writing in bold is for you. ADULTS: The rest is for you. Cut
the string off the chicken. Heat oven to 220C/200C fan/gas 7. Get your
child to use a pair of scissors to cut the elastic or string holding the
chicken together. 2Stuff the chicken. Stuff the lemon halves in the
cavity of the chicken with the garlic and herb sprig (if using). 3Time to
get your hands mucky. Sit the chicken in a large roasting tin and use
your hands to smear the butter all over it. 4 Easy-peasy vegetables. Tip
the carrots and potatoes into a large bowl, drizzle over the oil and toss
everything together with your hands.5 Scatter the vegetables around
the chicken. Scatter the vegetables in an even layer around the chicken,
then season everything. Put the chicken in the oven and roast for 30
mins. Remove from the oven and give the vegetables a stir, reduce the
heat to 200C/180C fan/gas 6, then return to the oven for 50 mins more.
6 Test if the chicken is cooked. Remove the chicken from the oven.
Using a cloth, pull the leg– if it easily comes away from the body, there
is no sign of pink and the juices run clear, the chicken is cooked. If you
have a digital cooking thermometer, it should read above 70C. Take the
chicken out of the tin. 7 Make a lemony sauce. Scoop the vegetables
into a serving dish. Using a spoon or a pair of tongs, remove the garlic,
lemon and herbs from the chicken and put them in the roasting tin.
Squash them down well with a potato masher to release all the juice
from the lemons. 8 Strain the sauce. Pour in the chicken stock and soy
sauce and give it all a good stir. Get the child to hold a sieve over a jug
while you lift up the pan and strain the juices into the jug. If you want
it piping hot, reheat in a pan or in the microwave

Notes:

15. Blueberry & lemon pancakes

• 200g plain flour• 1 tsp cream of tartar• ½ tsp bicarbonate of soda• 1 tsp golden syrup• 75g blueberry• zest 1 lemon• 200ml milk• 1 large egg• butter , for cooking

First, put the flour, cream of tartar and bicarbonate of soda in the bowl. Mix them well with the fork. Drop the golden syrup into the dry ingredients along with the blueberries and lemon zest. 2 Pour the milk into a measuring jug. Now break in the egg and mix well with a fork. Pour most of the milk mixture into the bowl and mix well with a rubber spatula. Keep adding more milk until you get a smooth, thick, pouring batter. 3 Heat the frying pan and brush with a little butter. Then spoon in the batter, 1 tbsp at a time, in heaps. Bubbles will appear on top as the pancakes cook— turn them at this stage, using the metal spatula to help you. Cook until brown on the second side, then keep warm on a plate, covered with foil. Repeat until all the mixture is used up.

Notes:

16. Chocolate fudge cupcakes

INGREDIENTS (12 Servings)

• 200g butter• 200g plain chocolate , under 70% cocoa solids is fine• 200g light, soft brown sugar• 2 eggs , beaten• 1 tsp vanilla extract• 250g self-raising flour• Smarties , sweets and sprinkles, to decorate For the icing • 200g plain chocolate• 100ml double cream , not fridge-cold• 50g icing sugar

DIRECTIONS (55 minutes)

Heat oven to 160C/140C fan/gas 3 and line a 12-hole muffin tin with cases. Gently melt the butter, chocolate, sugar and 100ml hot water together in a large saucepan, stirring occasionally, then set aside to cool a little while you weigh the other ingredients. 2 Stir the eggs and vanilla into the chocolate mixture. Put the flour into a large mixing bowl, then stir in the chocolate mixture until smooth. Spoon into cases until just over three-quarters full (you may have a little mixture leftover), then set aside for 5 mins before putting on a low shelf in the oven and baking for 20-22 mins. Leave to cool. 3 For the icing, melt the chocolate in a heatproof bowl over a pan of barely simmering water. Once melted, turn off the heat, stir in the double cream and sift in the icing sugar. When spreadable, top each cake with some and decorate with your favourite sprinkles and sweets.

Notes:

17. Cheese, ham & grape kebabs

• 6 bocconcini (mini mozzarella balls)• 6 grapes (a combination of red and green looks nice),• 6 cubes of ham

1 Using 3 short wooden skewers, thread on the mini mozzarella balls, grapes, and cubes of ham. Place in a sealable container or wrap in cling film and pop in a lunchbox. White rabbit biscuits

Notes:

18. Winter warmer hearty risotto

• 1 medium butternut squash• 2 tbsp olive oil• pinch of nutmeg ,
or pinch of cinnamon• 1 red onion , finely chopped• 1 vegetable
stock cube• 2 garlic cloves , crushed• 500g risotto rice (we used
arborio)• 100g frozen peas• 320g sweetcorn , drained• 2 tbsp
grated parmesan (or vegetarian alternative)• handful chopped
mixed herbs of your choice

DIRECTIONS (60 minutes)

1 Heat oven to 200C/180C fan/gas 6. Peel the butternut squash,
slice it in half, then scoop out and discard the seeds.2 Cut the
flesh of the butternut squash into small cubes and put in a mixing
bowl. Drizzle 1 tbsp olive oil over the squash, and season with
black pepper, and nutmeg or cinnamon. Transfer the squash to a
roasting tin and roast in the oven for about 25 mins until cooked
through, then set aside. 3Heat the remaining oil in a large
saucepan over a low heat. Add the onion and cover the pan with
a tight-fitting lid. Allow the onion to cook without colouring for
5-10 mins, stirring occasionally. 4 In a measuring jug, make up
1.5 litres of stock from boiling water and the stock cube. Stir well
until the stock cube has dissolved. When the onion is soft, remove
the lid and add the garlic to the onion pan. Leave it to cook for 1
min more. 5 Rinse the rice under cold water. Turn up the heat
on the pan and add the rice to the onion and garlic, stirring well
for 1 min. Pour a little of the hot stock into the pan and stir in until
the liquid is absorbed by the rice.Gradually add the rest of the
stock to the pan, a little at a time, stirring constantly, waiting until
each addition of stock is absorbed before adding more. Do this
until the rice is cooked through and creamy – you may not need
all the stock. This should take 15-20 mins. Take the roasting tin
out of the oven – the squash should be soft and cooked. 7 Add
the squash, peas and sweetcorn to the risotto and gently stir it in.
Season to taste. Take the risotto pan off the heat and stir in the
Parmesan and herbs. Put the lid back on the pan and let the
risotto stand for 2-3 mins before serving.

Notes:

19. Easy Makes Sushi

INGREDIENTS (6 Servings)

For the rice • 300g sushi rice• 100ml rice wine vinegar• 2 tbsp golden caster sugar For the Japanese mayonnaise • 3 tbsp mayonnaise• 1 tbsp rice wine vinegar• 1 tsp soy sauce For the sushi• 25g bag nori (seaweed) sheets• choose from the following fillings: cucumber strips, smoked salmon, white crabmeat, canned tuna, red pepper, avocado, spring onionTo serve with all styles of sushi • wasabi (optional - and fiery!)• pickled ginger• soy sauce

DIRECTIONS (55 minutes)

1 KIDS the writing in bold is for you. ADULTS the rest is for you. TO MAKE SUSHI ROLLS: Pat out some rice. Lay a nori sheet on the mat, shiny-side down. Dip your hands in the vinegared water, then pat handfuls of rice on top in a 1cm thick layer, leaving the furthest edge from you clear. 2Spread over some Japanese mayonnaise. Use a spoon to spread out a thin layer of mayonnaise down the middle of the rice. 3 Add the filling. Get your child to top the mayonnaise with a line of their favourite fillings – here we've used tuna and cucumber.4Roll it up. Lift the edge of the mat over the rice, applying a little pressure to keep everything in a tight roll 5Stick down the sides like a stamp. When you get to the edge without any rice, brush with a little water and continue to roll into a tight roll. Wrap in cling film. Remove the mat and roll tightly in cling film before a grown-up cuts the sushi into thick slices, then unravel the cling film.7 TO MAKE PRESSED SUSHI: Layerover some smoked salmon. Line a loaf tin with cling film, then place a thin layer of smoked salmon inside on top of the cling film.8Cover with rice and press down. Press about 3cm of rice over the fish, fold the cling film over and press down as much as you can, using another tin if you have one. 9Tip it out like a sandcastle. Turn block of sushi onto a chopping board. Get a grown-up to cut into fingers, then remove the cling film. 10 TO MAKE SUSHI BALLS: Choose your topping. Get a small square of cling film and place a topping, like half a prawn or a small piece of smoked salmon, on it. Use damp hands to roll walnutsized balls of rice and place on the topping. 11Make into tight balls. Bring the corners of the cling film together and tighten into balls by twisting it up, then unwrap and serve.

Notes:

20. Prawn & mango salad

• ½ avocado , peeled and cut into cubes, see tip, below left•
squeeze of lemon juice• 50g small cooked prawns• 1 mango
cheek, peeled and cut into cubes• 4 cherry tomatoes , halved•
finger-sized piece cucumber , chopped• handful baby spinach
leaves• couple of mint leaves , very finely shredded• 1-2 tsp
sweet chilli sauce

DIRECTIONS (10 minutes)

1 Mix the avocado with the lemon juice, then toss with the prawns,
mango, tomatoes, cucumber, spinach and mint. Pack into a
lunchbox and drizzle over the sweet chilli sauce, then chill until
ready to eat.

Notes:

21. Marshmallows dipped in chocolate

INGREDIENTS (26 Servings)

• 50g white chocolate• 50g milk chocolate• selection of cake sprinkles• 1 bag marshmallows (about 200g)• 1 pack lollipop sticks

DIRECTIONS (15 minutes)

1Heat the chocolate in separate bowls over simmering water or on a low setting in the microwave. Allow to cool a little. 2 Put your chosen sprinkles on separate plates. Push a cake pop or lolly stick into a marshmallow about half way in. Dip into the white or milk chocolate, allow the excess to drip off then dip into the sprinkles of your choice. Put into a tall glass to set. Repeat with each marshmallow.

Notes:

22. Bacon bolognese

• 400g spaghetti• 1 tsp olive oil• 2 large carrots , finely diced• 3 celery sticks, finely diced• 200g pack smoked bacon lardon• 190g jar sundried tomato pesto• 8-12 basil leaves , shredded (optional)

DIRECTIONS (22 minutes)

1 Boil the spaghetti following pack instructions. Meanwhile, heat the oil in a non-stick pan. Add the carrots, celery and bacon, and stir well. Cover the pan and cook, stirring occasionally, for 10 mins until the veg has softened. 2Tip in the pesto, warm through, then stir through the drained spaghetti with the basil, if using.

Notes:

23. Vanilla chick biscuit pops

• 200g unsalted butter , at room temperature• 100g golden caster sugar• 1 medium egg , beaten• 1 tsp vanilla extract• 200g plain flour , plus extra for dusting• 200g icing sugar• 2 tbsp milk• few drops yellow food colouring• 75g unsweetened desiccated coconut• 50g small chocolate chips• 25g orange or white fondant icing , plus a few drops orange food colouring You will need• 15-18 lolly sticks (see tip)• ribbon , to decorate (optional)

Put half the butter and all the sugar in a bowl. Using an electric whisk or wooden spoon, beat together until smooth and creamy. Beat in the egg and half the vanilla extract until thoroughly combined. 2 Tip the flour into the mixture and mix on a low speed until it comes together to form a dough. Gather up into a ball, wrap in cling film and chill in the fridge for 20 mins. 3 Heat oven to 180C/160C fan/gas 4. Line 2 baking trays with baking parchment. Put the biscuit dough on a lightly floured surface and roll out until about 5mm thick. Cut out the biscuits using a 6cm round cutter. Transfer the biscuits to the prepared trays and insert the lolly sticks into the sides, just a quarter of the way through. Bake for 6-7 mins until the edges are golden brown, then carefully transfer to a wire rack and allow to cool completely before decorating. 4 Meanwhile, make some buttercream frosting. Place the remaining softened butter in a bowl and beat with a wooden spoon. Slowly add the icing sugar, 1 tbsp at a time, until thoroughly incorporated and you have a smooth, creamy mixture. Add a little milk and the remaining vanilla extract with a few drops of food colouring to give a pale yellow colour. Chill for 5 mins. 5Put the desiccated coconut in a small bowl, add a few drops of yellow food colouring and mix well until the coconut is coloured pale yellow.6 Spread the buttercream frosting over one side of the biscuit and sprinkle with the coconut. Add 2 chocolate chip eyes to each. Pinch a little orange fondant icing and shape into a beak and press into the mixture. Decorate with a ribbon, if you like, and serve. Will keep for 2 days in an airtight container.

24. Christmas pudding Rice Krispie cakes

INGREDIENTS (12 Servings)

• 50g rice pops (we used Rice Krispies)• 30g raisin , chopped•
50g butter• 100g milk chocolate , broken into pieces• 2 tbsp
crunchy peanut butter• 30g mini marshmallow• 80g white
chocolate• ready-made icing holly leaves (we used Sainsbury's
Christmas cake decorations)

DIRECTIONS (30 hours 5 minutes)

1 Put the rice pops and raisins into a bowl. Put the butter, milk
chocolate, peanut butter and marshmallows into a small
saucepan. Place on a medium to low heat and stir until the
chocolate and butter have melted but the marshmallows are just
beginning to melt. 2 Pour onto the rice pops and stir until well
coated. Line an egg cup with cling film. Press about a tablespoon
of the mixture into the egg cup. Press firmly and then remove,
peel off the cling film and place the pudding into a cake case, flat-
side down. Repeat with the remaining mixture. Chill until firm.
3Melt the white chocolate in the microwave or in bowl over a
saucepan of barely simmering water. Spoon a little chocolate over
the top of each pudding. Top with icing holly leaves.

Notes:

25. Yummy chocolate log

For the cake • 3 eggs• 85g golden caster sugar• 85g plain flour (minus 2 tbsp)• 2 tbsp cocoa powder• ½ tsp baking powder For the filling & icing • 50g butter, plus extra for the tin• 140g dark chocolate , broken into squares• 1 tbsp golden syrup• 284ml pot double cream• 200g icing sugar, sifted• 2-3 extra strong mints, crushed (optional)• icing sugar and holly sprigs to decorate - ensure you remove the berries before serving

1 Heat the oven to 200C/180C fan/gas 6. Butter and line a 23 x 32cm Swiss roll tin with baking parchment. Beat the eggs and golden caster sugar together with an electric whisk for about 8 mins until thick and creamy. 2 Mix the flour, cocoa powder and baking powder together, then sift onto the egg mixture. Fold in very carefully, then pour into the tin. Tip the tin from side to side to spread the mixture into the corners. Bake for 10 mins. 3 Lay a sheet of baking parchment on a work surface. When the cake is ready, tip it onto the parchment, peel off the lining paper, then roll the cake up from its longest edge with the paper inside. Leave to cool. 4 To make the icing, melt the butter and dark chocolate together in a bowl over a pan of hot water. Take from the heat and stir in the golden syrup and 5 tbsp double cream. Beat in the icing sugar until smooth. 5 Whisk the remaining double cream until it holds its shape. Unravel the cake, spread the cream over the top, scatter over the crushed extra strong mints, if using, then carefully roll up again into a log.6 Cut a thick diagonal slice from one end of the log. Lift the log on to a plate, then arrange the slice on the side with the diagonal cut against the cake to make a branch. Spread the icing over the log and branch (don't cover the ends), then use a fork to mark the icing to give the effect of tree bark. Scatter with unsifted icing sugar to resemble snow, and decorate with holly.

Notes:

26. Easy Easter nests

• 200g milk chocolate , broken into pieces• 85g shredded wheat , crushed• 2 x 100g bags mini chocolate eggs You'll also need • cupcake cases

DIRECTIONS (31 minutes)

1 Melt the chocolate in a small bowl placed over a pan of barely simmering water. Pour the chocolate over the shredded wheat and stir well to combine. 2 Spoon the chocolate wheat into 12 cupcake cases and press the back of a teaspoon in the centre to create a nest shape. Place 3 mini chocolate eggs on top of each nest. Chill the nests in the fridge for 2 hrs until set.

Notes:

27. No-fuss fish pie

INGREDIENTS (4 Servings)

• 400ml milk• 1 bay leaf• 1 garlic clove , finely chopped• 1 medium onion , thinly sliced• 300g skinless, boneless fish (we used a mix of salmon, smoked haddock and cod) • 5 medium potatoes• 3 parsnips , peeled• 2 eggs• 125g (drained weight) can sweetcorn• 125g frozen peas• 2 tbsp mixed chopped herbs (lemon thyme, coriander and chives are nice)• zest 0.5 lemon• small pack of cooked small prawns (optional)• 4 tsp crème fraîche• pinch of ground nutmeg• pinch of white pepper• 1 tsp wholegrain mustard• 25g butter• 50g grated cheese• steamed carrots , to serve• steamed broccoli , to serve

DIRECTIONS (55 minutes)

1 Heat oven to 190C/170C fan/gas 5. Put the milk in a saucepan with the bay leaf, garlic and onion. Add the fish and poach on a medium heat for 15 mins. The milk should be just covering the fish, if not, add a little more. 2 Cut the potatoes and parsnips into equal-sized pieces and put in a saucepan. Cover with cold water and a lid, bring to the boil, then simmer on a medium heat for 10 mins, or until the potatoes and parsnips are soft (not falling apart). 3 Meanwhile, gently put the eggs in a small pan of water and bring to the boil. Cook for 7 mins, then transfer to a bowl of cold water and leave to cool. Once cool, peel and chop them. 4When the fish is cooked (it should be firm to the touch and flake easily), remove from the milk, along with the onion, using a slotted spoon. Strain the milk into a jug and keep it for the mash.5Flake the fish into bite-sized chunks (checking for bones) and place in the bottom of a casserole dish, then add the onion, sweetcorn and peas.6Add the herbs, lemon zest, prawns (if using), hard-boiled eggs and the crème fraîche. Season and mix well.7Drain the parsnips and potatoes in a colander, and return to the saucepan. Add the nutmeg, white pepper, mustard and a knob of butter and mash well 8Taste to check the seasoning. Cover the fish filling with the mashed potato and, using a fork, create a wavy pattern, if you like. Sprinkle over the grated cheese.9Place in the oven for 20 mins or until the cheese is melted and golden brown, remove from the oven using oven gloves and serve with steamed crunchy carrots and broccoli.

Notes:

28. Carrot cake traybake

INGREDIENTS (6 Servings)

• 200g carrots , peeled• 175g soft brown sugar• 200g self-raising flour• 1 tsp bicarbonate of soda• 2 tsp cinnamon• zest 1 orange• 2 eggs• 150ml sunflower oil For the icing • 50g softened butter• 75g icing sugar• 200g soft cheese• sprinkles (optional)

DIRECTIONS (60 minutes)

1 Line an 18cm square tin with baking parchment. Ask your grown-up helper to turn the oven on to 180C/160C fan/gas 2. Grate the carrots on the fine side of the grater, then tip them into a large bowl. 2 Sift the sugar, flour, bicarb and cinnamon on top of the carrot, then add the orange zest and mix everything around a bit. 3Break the eggs into a bowl (scoop out any bits of shell), then add them to the bowl along with the oil. Mix everything together well 4Scoop the cake mix into your tin and level the top. Ask a grown-up to put it in the oven for 30 minutes or until the cake is cooked. Cool. 5To make the icing, mix the butter and icing sugar together, then stir in the soft cheese until smooth.6When the cake is cool, spread the top with the icing and cut into squares. Decorate with sprinkles, if you like.

29. Choco-dipped tangerines

• 1 tangerine , peeled and segmented• 10g dark chocolate , melted

DIRECTIONS (10 minutes)

1 Dip half of each tangerine segment in the melted chocolate, then put on a baking sheet lined with parchment. Keep in the fridge for 1 hr to set completely, or overnight if you prefer.

Notes:

30. Chocolate crunch bars Cook

• 100g butter , roughly chopped• 300g dark chocolate (such as Bournville), broken into squares• 3 tbsp golden syrup• 140g rich tea biscuit , roughly crushed• 12 pink marshmallows , quartered (use scissors)• 2 x 55g bars Turkish delight , halved and sliced (or use Maltesers, Milky Way or Crunchie bars)

DIRECTIONS (20 minutes)

1 Gently melt the butter, chocolate and syrup in a pan over a low heat, stirring frequently until smooth, then cool for about 10 mins. 2 Stir the biscuits and sweets into the pan until well mixed, then pour into a 17cm square tin lined with foil and spread the mixture to roughly level it. Chill until hard, then cut into fingers.

Notes:

31. Fruity Neapolitan lolly loaf

INGREDIENTS (8 Servings)

• 200g peaches nectarines or apricots (or a mixture), stoned• 200g strawberries or raspberries (or a mixture), hulled• 450ml double cream• ½ x 397g can condensed milk• 2 tsp vanilla extract• orange and pink food colouring (optional)• 8 wooden lolly sticks

DIRECTIONS (8 hours 50 minutes)

1 Put the peaches, nectarines or apricots in a food processor and pulse until they're chopped and juicy but still with some texture. Scrape into a bowl. Repeat with the berries and scrape into another bowl. 2 Pour the cream, condensed milk and vanilla into a third bowl and whip until just holding soft peaks. Add roughly a third of the mixture to the peaches and another third to the berries, and mix both until well combined. Add a drop of orange food colouring to the peach mixture and a drop of pink food colouring to the berry mixture if you want a really vibrant colour. Line a 900g loaf tin or terrine mould with cling film (look for a long thin one, ours was 23 x 7 x 8cm), then pour in the berry mixture. Freeze for 2 hrs and chill the remaining mixtures in the fridge. 3 Once the bottom layer is frozen, remove the vanilla mixture from the fridge and pour over the berry layer. The bottom layer should now be firm enough to support your lolly sticks, so place these, evenly spaced, along the length of the loaf tin, pushing down gently until they stand up straight. Return to the freezer for another 2 hrs. 4 4 Once the vanilla layer is frozen, pour over the peach mixture, easing it around the lolly sticks. Return to the freezer for a further 4 hrs or until completely frozen. Remove from the freezer 10 mins before serving. Use the cling film to help you remove the loaf from the tin. Take to the table on a board and slice off individual lollies for your guests. Any leftovers can be kept in the freezer for up to 2 weeks.

Notes:

32. Crisp chicken bites

• 4 boneless chicken breast fillets• 6 tbsp red pesto• 3 large handfuls breadcrumbs , frsh or dried (about 300g/10oz)• olive oil

1 Cut the chicken breasts into small chunks, each about the size of a marble (you should get roughly 15 pieces per breast). Put the pesto in a bowl and mix together with the chicken until coated all over. Tip the breadcrumbs into a large freezer bag. 2 Add the chicken pieces in batches to the bag and give it a good shake to coat. Place a piece of greaseproof paper on a baking sheet, then lay the chicken pieces on the sheet, making sure none of them are touching. Put in the freezer and, when frozen solid, take off the baking sheet and store in a container or freezer bag. 3 To cook, heat oven to 220C/fan 200C/ gas 7. Pour a little oil onto a shallow baking tray, just enough to cover it. Put the tray in the oven and let it heat up for 5 mins. Tip the chicken onto the sheet and return to the oven for 10-15 mins until crisp and cooked through.

Notes:

33. Stuffed jacket potatoes

INGREDIENTS (6 Servings)

4 medium potatoes• 100g strong cheddar, grated, plus extra for topping• 100g sweetcorn• 100g mixed pepper, diced• small handful fresh herbs, such as oregano, basil, coriander, dill or thyme

DIRECTIONS (1 hour 35 minutes)

1 Equipment you will need: medium mixing bowl, small mixing bowl, dessertspoon, fork, baking tray, grater, oven gloves.2Get an adult to heat the oven to 200C/180C fan/gas 6 and bake the potatoes for about 1 hr until cooked and the skins are crispy. Leave to cool completely. This can be done up to 2 days ahead. 3 To stuff the jacket potatoes, heat the oven to 200C/180C fan/gas 6. Ask an adult to cut the potatoes in half. Using a spoon, carefully scoop out the middle of the potato, leaving the skin unbroken (like a boat). Place the scooped potato into a mixing bowl. 4 Using the fork, mash the potato until there are no lumps. Add the cheese, sweetcorn and peppers and mix well. Gently pick the leaves from the herbs. You can rip the larger leaves into smaller pieces. Stir the herbs into the cheesy potato mixture. 5 Using the spoon, carefully scoop the mixture back into the potato boats. Make sure that you use all the mixture up. Sprinkle with a little extra grated cheese and place on a baking tray. Using oven gloves, place the tray in the oven and bake for 10-15 mins until golden.

Notes:

34. Millionaire's chocolate tart

• 375g pack dessert shortcrust pastry• 1 tsp vanilla paste or extract• flour , for dusting• 250g/9oz caramel (we used Carnation caramel from a can)• 100g 70% plain chocolate , broken into pieces• 100g white chocolate , broken into pieces• 6 tbsp melted butter• 2 eggs , plus 3 egg yolks• 4 tbsp golden caster sugar• icing sugar and single cream, to serve (optional)

1 Break the pastry into chunks and drop into a food processor. Drizzle over the vanilla paste and pulse until the vanilla is speckled through the pastry (the extract should be completely absorbed). Tip out onto a floured surface, bring together into a ball, then roll out to line a 23cm tart tin (leave any overhanging pastry as you will trim this away when the tart is baked). Chill for 30 mins. 2 Heat oven to 200C/180C fan/gas 6. Line the pastry with greaseproof paper. Fill with baking beans, bake blind for 15-20 mins, then remove the paper and beans and bake for 5-10 mins more until pale golden. Carefully spread caramel over the base and set aside while you make the filling. Lower oven to 180C/160C fan/gas 4. 3 Melt the chocolates in a bowl over a pan of barely simmering water, then stir in the melted butter. Whisk the eggs, yolks and sugar together with an electric whisk in a large mixing bowl for 10 mins, until pale and thick enough to leave a trail when the beaters are lifted up. Fold in the melted chocolate with a large metal spoon, then scrape into the tin. 4Bake for 20-25 mins – the surface should be set and puffed but still with a slight wobble. Cool, then chill for at least 3 hrs or overnight, before dusting with icing sugar and serving.

Notes:

35. Eyeball & hand fruit punch

INGREDIENTS (15 Servings)

• 425g can lychees• 225g jar cocktail cherries• 15 raisins• 1 litre carton blueberry, blackberry or purple grape juice , chilled• 1 litre carton cherry or cranberry juice , chilled• 1litre sparkling water , chilled You'll also need • 2 pairs powder-free disposable gloves

DIRECTIONS (10 minutes)

1 Rinse the disposable gloves and fill each with water. Tie a knot in the top of each as you would a balloon, or use a tight bag clip to hold the opening closed. Freeze overnight.2Drain the lychees and cocktail cherries, reserving the juices in a jug. Push a raisin into one end of each cherry, then push the cherries into the lychees to make 'eyeballs'.3 Tip all of the juices, plus the reserved lychee and cherry juices, into a large bowl with the 'eyeballs'. Carefully peel the gloves from the ice hands, add to the punch, then top up with the sparkling water.

Notes:

36. Rudolph cupcakes

INGREDIENTS (12 Servings)

• 200g butter , cubed• 200g plain chocolate , broken into squares• 200g light soft brown sugar• 2 large eggs , beaten• 1 tsp vanilla extract• 250g self-raising flour For the icing • 200g plain chocolate , broken into squares• 100ml double cream , not fridge-cold• 50g icing sugar For the reindeers • 12 large milk chocolate buttons (we used Cadbury Dairy Milk Giant Buttons)• 24 white chocolate buttons• 12 red Smarties• black icing pens• mini pretzels , carefully cut in half horizontally

DIRECTIONS (55 minutes)

1 Get started: Heat oven to 160C/140C fan/gas 3. Line a 12-hole muffin tin with paper cases. Gently melt the butter, chocolate, sugar and 100ml hot water together in a large saucepan, stirring occasionally. Set aside to cool a little while you weigh the other ingredients. 2 Make your cakes: Stir the eggs and vanilla into the chocolate mixture. Put the flour in a large mixing bowl, and stir in the chocolate mixture until smooth. Spoon into the cases until just over three-quarters full. Bake on a low shelf in the oven for 20-22 mins. Leave to cool. 3 Ice the tops: To make the icing, melt the chocolate in a heatproof bowl over a pan of barely simmering water. Once melted, turn off the heat, stir in the double cream, sift in the icing sugar and mix well. When spreadable, top each cake with some icing. 4 Have fun decorating: Position a milk chocolate button on top of each cake, then 2 white chocolate buttons above it. Use a little icing as glue to stick a red Smartie onto the milk chocolate button for a nose. Then use your icing pens to draw black dots on the white buttons for eyes. Stick 2 pretzel top halves into the top of each cake for antlers, and stick the bottom half of a pretzel under the Smartie for a mouth. These cakes will keep in a sealed container for up to 3 days, but we doubt they'll last that long!

Notes:

37. Stripy hummus salad jars

• 140g frozen soya beans or peas• 200g tub hummus (reserve 2 tbsp for the dressing)• 2 red peppers (or a mixture of colours) finely chopped• Half cucumber , finely chopped• 200g cherry tomatoes , quartered• 2 large carrots• small pack basil• 2 large carrots , peeled and grated• 4 tbsp pumpkin seeds (optional) For the dressing • zest and juice 1 lemon• 1 tbsp clear honey• 2 tbsp hummus (from the tub, above)

DIRECTIONS (15 minutes)

1 First make the dressing. Put the ingredients in a jam jar with 1 tbsp water. Screw on the lid and shake well. Set aside. 2 Bring a small pan of water to the boil, add the beans or peas and cook for 1 min until tender. Drain and run under cold water until cool. Divide the remaining hummus between 6 large jam jars. Top with the drained soya beans or peas, peppers, cucumber, tomatoes, basil leaves, carrots and pumpkin seeds, if using. Screw on the lids and chill until needed. Will keep in the fridge for 24 hrs. 3 When ready to serve, pass around the jars and let everyone pour over a little dressing.

Notes:

38. Toffee popcorn bark

INGREDIENTS (8 Servings)

• 200g milk chocolate• 200g white chocolate• x bags toffee popcorn

DIRECTIONS (15 minutes)

1 Line a 20 x 30cm baking tray with baking parchment. Melt the milk chocolate and white chocolate separately, then allow to cool slightly. 2 Pour most of the chocolate onto the tray, roughly swirling together. Sprinkle over the toffee popcorn, then drizzle over the remaining milk and white chocolate, and chill until set. Break into big chunks before serving.

Notes:

39. Rigatoni sausage bake

• 400g good quality pork sausage• 1 tbsp olive oil• 1 onion, chopped• 1 large carrot, grated• 150ml red wine• 300ml vegetable stock• 3 tbsp tomato purée For the sauce • 50g butter• 50g plain flour• 600ml milk• freshly grated nutmeg• 500g rigatoni or penne• 200g fresh spinach• 140g mature cheddar, grated

DIRECTIONS (1 hour 50 minutes)

1 Slit the sausages and remove them from their skins, then chop them into small pieces. Heat the oil in a pan, add the onion and fry for 5 minutes, until softened and lightly browned. Stir in the sausages and fry until lightly coloured. Add the carrot, then stir in the wine, stock, tomato purée, and season. 2Bring to the boil, then simmer uncovered for about 15 minutes until thickened. Taste and season. Set aside. 3Put the butter, flour and milk in a pan. Gently heat, whisking, until thickened and smooth. Add a sprinkle of freshly grated nutmeg, season, then simmer for 2 minutes. 4 Preheat the oven to 190C/Gas 5/fan 170C. Bring a large pan of salted water to the boil. Add the pasta, stir well, then cook, uncovered, for 10-12 minutes, until tender. Remove from the heat, stir in the spinach and, when just wilted, drain well. 5 Tip half the pasta into a shallow ovenproof dish, about 2.2 litre/4 pint, and level. Spoon over the sausage sauce, then cover with the remaining pasta. Pour the white sauce evenly over the top and sprinkle with the cheddar. Bake for 20-25 minutes until golden brown. Leave for 5 minutes before serving.

Notes:

40. Shimmering forest cake

To cover the cake • 20cm/8inch round fruitcake• 3 tbsp apricot jam , warmed• icing sugar , for dusting• 750g natural-coloured marzipan• 750g white ready-to-roll icing To decorate • 500g white ready-to-roll icing• green food colouring paste• 200g icing sugar , plus extra for dusting• 2Christmas tree cutters , about 5cm and 10cm tall• 1 egg white• edible sparkles , available from cookshops• green Smarties and silver chocolate buttons (optional)

1Cover the cake with marzipan and white icing. (See 5 for more information). 2 Knead the ready-to-roll icing, then split into three balls. Leave one ball white, and knead a little green colouring into the other two to give two different shades of green. Roll out each ball to about 5mm thick on a work surface lightly dusted with icing sugar. Stamp out about 15 tree shapes using tree cutters, then leave to dry for a few hours or overnight.Once firm, lift half of the trees onto a cooling rack. Combine the 200g icing sugar and egg white to make an icing, then drizzle it over the trees with a teaspoon. Scatter with edible sparkles and leave to dry again until solid. 4 Put a little icing on the back of each tree and press the trees around the edge of the cake, overlapping some to give a 3-D effect. Scatter the sweets over the top of the cake to finish. Can be iced up to a week ahead. 5 To cover a cake with marzipan, first brush the cake all over with a thin layer of warmed apricot jam. Dust the work surface with icing sugar, then roll out the marzipan evenly until you have a 5mm1cm thick round, about 40cm across for a 20cm cake. Lift over the cake, using a rolling pin to help, then smooth with your hands and trim off the excess. Leave to dry overnight or for a few hours. Lightly brush the marzipan all over with cooled, boiled water. Roll the icing out as you did the marzipan, then smooth with your hands, trim off the excess and leave to dry.

Notes:

41. Asian chicken salad

• 1 boneless, skinless chicken breast• 1 tbsp fish sauce• zest and juice ½ lime (about 1 tbsp)• 1 tsp caster sugar• 100g bag mixed salad leaves• large handful coriander , roughly chopped• ¼ red onion , thinly sliced• ½ chilli , deseeded and thinly sliced• ¼ cucumber , halved lengthways, sliced

DIRECTIONS (20 minutes)

1 Cover the chicken with cold water, bring to the boil, then cook for 10 mins. Remove from the pan and tear into shreds. Stir together the fish sauce, lime zest, juice and sugar until sugar dissolves. 2Place the leaves and coriander in a container, then top with the chicken, onion, chilli and cucumber. Place the dressing in a separate container and toss through the salad when ready to eat.

Notes:

42. Cheeseburgers

INGREDIENTS (12 Servings)

• 1kg minced beef• 300g breadcrumbs• 140g extra-mature or mature cheddar , grated• 4 tbsp Worcestershire sauce• 1 small bunch parsley , finely chopped• 2 eggs , beaten To serve • split burger buns• sliced tomatoes• red onion slices• lettuce , tomato sauce, coleslaw, wedges or fries

DIRECTIONS (35 minutes)

1 Crumble the mince in a large bowl, then tip in the breadcrumbs, cheese, Worcestershire sauce, parsley and eggs with 1 tsp ground pepper and 1-2 tsp salt. Mix with your hands to combine everything thoroughly. 2 Shape the mix into 12 burgers. Chill until ready to cook for up to 24 hrs. Or freeze for up to 3 months. Just stack between squares of baking parchment to stop the burgers sticking together, then wrap well. Defrost overnight in the fridge before cooking. 3 To cook the burgers, heat grill to high. Grill burgers for 6-8 mins on each side until cooked through. Meanwhile, warm as many buns as you need in a foil-covered tray below the grilling burgers. Let everyone assemble their own, served with their favourite accompaniments.

Notes:

43. Fish cake fingers

• 800g floury potato• 2 skinless salmon fillets (about 250g), cut into chunks • 3 smoked mackerel fillets (about 140g)• zest 1 lemon , saving juice to serve• plain flour , for dusting• 3 eggs• 100g dried breadcrumb• 3 tbsp sunflower oil , plus more if needed To serve • 6 tbsp mayonnaise• lemon juice , from above• 1 small garlic clove , chopped (optional)• 200g frozen pea , cooked• few handfuls watercress

1 KIDS: The writing in bold is for you GROWN-UPS: The rest is for you. Make some mash. Tip the potatoes into a pan of cold water and bring to the boil. Boil for 10 mins then lower the heat and drop in the salmon. Turn down the heat and simmer for about 3-5 mins more until the fish is cooked. Lift the fish onto a plate with a slotted spoon. Continue cooking the potatoes until soft, then drain. Tip the potatoes into a bowl and get your child to mash them. 2Flake the fish. While the potatoes cook, peel away the skin from the mackerel fillets and get your child to flake the meat into a small bowl – they can taste some at this point, if they like. 3 Mix it all up. Add the lemon zest to the potato, and mash some more. Then add all the flaked fish and mix together well – don't worry about breaking up the fish. If you want, divide the mix in half and add any grown-up ingredients at this stage. Leave until cool enough to handle. 4 Roll out into long sausages. Lightly flour a surface and crack the eggs into a dish. Get your child to whisk them while you tip the breadcrumbs into another dish. Then ask them to divide the mash into eight and roll them on the flour into long, fat cylinders. 5Dip them in egg. Working methodically, roll the sausages carefully in the egg. 6 Coat in crunchy breadcrumbs. Once the sausages are completely coated in egg, roll them in the Once the sausages are completely coated in egg, roll them in the 3 days, or frozen for 1 month. To cook from frozen, Heat oven to 180C/160C fan/gas 4. Drizzle some olive oil over the Fish cake fingers and bake for 25-30 mins, until cooked through and golden. 7 Get a grown-up to cook them. Heat the oil in a frying pan and cook the fingers in batches. Sizzle them for 8-10 mins, turning regularly until completely golden, then lift them out onto kitchen paper to drain. Keep them warm in a low oven while you cook the rest. 8 Make a tasty sauce. While you are cooking the fingers, your child can mix the mayonnaise with the lemon juice and garlic – then get them to tip it into a small dish. Serve the fish cake fingers on a plate with the peas, watercress and some of the mayonnaise dip on the side.

Notes:

44. Cauliflower cheese pasta bake

INGREDIENTS (4 Servings)

• 1 cauliflower , broken down into florets, core sliced, leaves removed and reserved, thick stems sliced• 2 tbsp olive oil• 6 shallots , sliced• 1 tsp caster sugar• 1 thyme sprig• 2 tbsp white wine• 100g large pasta shapes, such as conchiglioni• 20g butter• 1 bay leaf• 2 tbsp plain flour• 600ml milk• 100g mature cheddar• 50g parmesan (or vegetarian alternative), plus extra to top• nutmeg , grated• 50g gruyère or comté• 1 tsp white wine vinegar or lemon juice

DIRECTIONS (1 hour 20 minutes)

1 Heat oven to 220C/200 fan/gas 9. Toss the cauliflower florets, leaves and sliced core with 1 tbsp olive oil in a roasting tin and season. Roast in the oven for 30-40 mins, or until the cauliflower is turning golden and smelling nutty. While it's roasting, heat 1 tbsp of olive oil in a non-stick frying pan and add the shallots, sugar and thyme. Cook for 10-15 mins until soft, sweet and caramelised. Add the wine and cook for a few more mins until evaporated. Meanwhile, cook the pasta in salty boiling water until just cooked. Drain and set aside. 2 For the cheese sauce, melt the butter in a non-stick saucepan over a medium heat with the bay leaf. Add the flour and cook, stirring, for 2 mins or so, until the roux is starting to bubble. Pour in the milk, little by little, stirring with a whisk, until fully incorporated and you have a smooth, lump-free sauce. Cook for about 10 mins until thickened, and then season with nutmeg and black pepper. Next, add the cheese and stir over the heat until it's melted and smooth. Taste the sauce and adjust the seasoning, adding the vinegar or lemon juice to taste. 3 Tip the pasta and shallots into the cauliflower roasting dish, then pour over the cheese sauce and stir so everything is well coated. Sprinkle over the remaining parmesan, reduce the oven to 180C/160C fan/gas 4 and bake for 20 mins, or until golden. Remove from the oven and allow to settle for about 10 mins, then serve with a crisp chicory salad.

Notes:

45. Lemony Easter chicks

• 2 medium egg whites• 100g golden caster sugar• ½ tsp cornflour• grated zest 1/2 lemon , plus 1 tsp juice• yellow food colouring paste• orange, black and yellow icing pen , to decorate

Heat oven to 140C/120C fan/gas 1. Line a baking sheet with baking parchment and put a mediumsized plain nozzle on a piping bag.2In a clean bowl, whisk the egg whites until they are very stiff. Add half the sugar and continue to whisk until the mixture is becoming firm and shiny. 3 Stir the cornflour into the remaining sugar and add to the meringue, along with the lemon zest and juice, and a smidge of yellow food colouring paste. Whisk again until you have a very thick, firm and glossy pale yellow meringue. 4 Carefully spoon the meringue into the piping bag. Push any air out of the top and tightly twist the opening to seal. Pipe about 25 thumb-sized dollops onto your baking sheet – if possible, try to make them wider at the base than the top, resembling a chick's body and head. Leave a gap between each chick to allow for expanding when cooking. 5Cook in the oven for 30 mins until they are crisp, firm and come off the baking parchment easily. Leave to cool on a wire rack. 6 To decorate, use the orange icing pen to make a V-shaped beak, and a black icing pen for eyes and feet. The yellow icing pen can be used to decorate fluffy hair on the chick's head and/or wings. Will keep for up to 1 week in an airtight container.

Notes:

46. Mini chocolate cheesecakes

INGREDIENTS (12 Servings)

14 milk chocolate digestive biscuits , finely crushed• 100g butter , meltedFor the filling • 500g tub ricotta• 3 eggs , beaten• 1 tsp vanilla extract• 200g cheap dark chocolate , broken into chunks and melted• 125g icing sugar• 36 mini chocolate eggs

DIRECTIONS (50 minutes)

1 Heat oven to 150C/130C fan/gas 2. Line the holes of a muffin tin with 12 paper muffin cases. Put the biscuits in a food bag and bash to small crumbs with the end of a rolling pin. Tip into a bowl, stir in the melted butter until the crumbs are nicely coated, then spoon between the paper cases. Press down into the bottoms to make a firm base. 2 To make the filling, put the ricotta, eggs, vanilla and melted chocolate in a large mixing bowl. Sift in the icing sugar. Beat everything together with an electric whisk or a wooden spoon until very well combined. Spoon into the paper cases right up to the tops, then tap the whole tin on the bench to get rid of any air bubbles. Bake for 30 mins, then remove from the oven and gently push 3 mini eggs into the top of each cheesecake. Let the cheesecakes cool completely before serving. Can be kept in the fridge for up to 3 days.

Notes:

47. Christmas pudding cake pops

• 200g madeira cake• 140g-160g white chocolate (see Tip)• 1 orange , zest finely grated To decorate • 300g dark chocolate , 60-70% cocoa solids, broken into chunks• 50g white chocolate , broken into chunks• sugar holly decorations or red and green writing icing

1 Pulse the madeira cake in a food processor until you have fine crumbs. Melt the white chocolate in a bowl over just simmering water or in the microwave. Shop bought madeira cake can vary in texture so you may need to add a little extra melted white chocolate to make the mixture stick into balls. Stir the orange zest into the chocolate, then work the chocolate into the crumbs using your hands. 2 Form into 10 small truffle-sized balls, then roll gently in your palms to smooth the surface. Arrange the balls on a baking parchment-lined dinner plate. Refrigerate for 30 minutes to allow the mixture to set. 3 Melt the dark chocolate in a microwave or over a bowl of just simmering water. Dip a lolly stick into the melted chocolate about 1.5cm in and poke half way into a cake ball. Repeat with the remaining balls. Put them back on the plate. Return to the fridge for five minutes. 4 Dip the cake pops one at a time into the melted chocolate, allowing any excess chocolate to drip off and spin the pops to even out the surface. Poke the pops into a piece of polystyrene or cake pop holder if you have one, keeping the pops apart. Allow to set for about half an hour. 5 Heat the white chocolate in a microwave or over a pan of simmering water. Allow to cool for a few minutes until it has a thick, runny consistency. If the chocolate is too hot, it will melt the dark chocolate underneath so make sure you do not overheat it. Spoon a small amount on top of the cake pops and tip them back and forth so that it runs down the sides a little. If you have holly decorations, set one on each pop. If using writing icing, wait for another 20 minutes or so until the white chocolate has set. To avoid a bloom on the chocolate, cover the cake pops in chocolate on the day you want to eat them– or the day before at the earliest. 6Pipe on holly leaves with the green icing and two little dots for berries using the red. Once finished, store them in a cool place, though not the fridge

Notes:

48. Creamy veggie risotto

• 1 tbsp olive oil• 1 onion , chopped• 1 parsnip , finely diced• 2 medium carrots , finely diced• 350g risotto rice , such as arborio• 1 bay leaf• 1.2l hot vegetable or chicken stock• 140g frozen pea or petit pois• 50g parmesan (or vegetarian alternative), grated

1 Heat the oil in a large shallow pan. Tip in the onion, parsnip and carrots, cover and gently fry for 8 mins until the onion is very soft.2 Stir in the rice and bay leaf, then gently fry for another 2-3 mins until the rice starts to turn seethrough around the edges. Add 300ml of the stock and simmer over a gentle heat, stirring until it has all been absorbed. Carry on adding the hot stock, a ladleful at a time, letting it be absorbed before adding more. Continue until the rice is just cooked and all the stock has been used, adding a little more water or stock if needed. This will take 18-20 mins. 3Remove the bay leaf from the cooked risotto and stir in the peas. Heat through for a few mins, then add most of the Parmesan and season to taste. Sprinkle with the remaining Parmesan and serve.

Notes:

49. Pumpkin risotto

• 1 small pumpkin or butternut squash- after peeling and scraping out the seeds, you need about 400g/14oz• 1 tbsp olive oil, plus a drizzle for the pumpkin• 2 garlic cloves• 8 spring onions• 25g butter• 200g risotto rice• 2 tsp ground cumin• 1l hot vegetable stock, plus extra splash if needed• 50g grated parmesan (or vegetarian alternative)• small handful coriander, roughly chopped

DIRECTIONS (1 hour 30 minutes)

1 Heat oven to 180C/160C fan/ gas 4. Chop up the pumpkin or squash into 1.5cm cubes (kids- ask for help if it's slippery). Put it on a baking tray, drizzle over some oil, then roast for 30 mins. 2 While the pumpkin is roasting, you can make the risotto. Put the garlic in a sandwich bag, then bash lightly with a rolling pin until it's crushed. 3Cut up the spring onions with your scissors. 4 Heat 1 tbsp oil with the butter in your pan over a medium heat – not too hot. Add the spring onions and garlic. Once the onions are soft but not getting brown, add the rice and cumin. Stir well to coat in the buttery mix for about 1 min. 5 Now add half a cup of the stock, and stir every now and then until it has all disappeared into the rice. Carry on adding and stirring in a large splash of stock at a time, until you have used up all the stock– this will take about 20 mins. 6 Check the rice is cooked. If it isn't, add a splash more stock, and carry on cooking for a bit. Once the rice is soft enough to eat, gently stir in the grated cheese, chopped coriander and roasted pumpkin.

Notes:

50. Spicy meatballs

INGREDIENTS (6 Servings)

• 500g minced chicken , turkey, lamb, beef or pork• 1 medium onion• 2 garlic cloves , crushed or chopped• 2 tsp mild or medium curry powder• 2 tsp ground cumin• 1 tsp garam masala• ½ tsp paprika or cayenne pepper• 2 tbsp fresh coriander , chopped• 1 egg , beaten• 50g fresh breadcrumb• 1 tbsp olive oil

DIRECTIONS (40 minutes)

1Heat oven to 180C/fan 160C/gas 4. 2 Put the mince into the mixing bowl. Add the onions, garlic, curry powder, cumin, garam masala, paprika or cayenne pepper and coriander, then mix well. By adding these spices, you'll get a delicious flavour without having to add any salt. 3Add the beaten egg and breadcrumbs, then mix again.4 Divide the meat mixture into 15-18 evensized pieces and shape into balls (they should be about the size of a walnut). Always wash your hands thoroughly after handling raw meat so you don't transfer any germs that may be on the meat to other food or equipment. 5 Heat the oil in the frying pan over a medium heat and add the meatballs using a spoon. Cook them for 5 mins, turning until golden brown. Remove from the pan and place them on to the tray. Bake in the oven for 15-20 mins. 6 Remove from the oven. Remember to use oven gloves! Allow to cool slightly and serve with a fresh, crisp green salad, some pitta bread and tomato salsa.

Notes:

51. Vietnamese veggie hotpot

• 2 tsp vegetable oil• thumb-size piece fresh root ginger ,
shredded• 2 garlic cloves , chopped• ½ large butternut squash ,
peeled and cut into chunks• 2 tsp soy sauce• 2 tsp soft brown
sugar• 200ml vegetable stock• 100g green bean , trimmed and
sliced• 4 spring onions , sliced• coriander leaves and cooked
basmati or jasmine rice, to serve

1 Heat the oil in a medium-size, lidded saucepan. Add the ginger
and garlic, then stir-fry for about 5 mins. Add the squash, soy
sauce, sugar and stock. Cover, then simmer for 10 mins. Remove
the lid, add the green beans, then cook for 3 mins more until the
squash and beans are tender. Stir the spring onions through at
the last minute, then sprinkle with coriander and serve with rice.

Notes:

52. Baileys banana trifles

• 300g pot extra-thick double cream• 7 tbsp Baileys• 6 chocolate brownies (about 250g/9oz), broken up, or use crumbled chocolate biscuits or loaf cake• 3 bananas , sliced• 500g pot vanilla custard• 6 tbsp toffee sauce• 25g chocolate , grated

DIRECTIONS (10 minutes)

1 Mix the cream with 1 tbsp Baileys, and set aside. Divide the brownie pieces between 6 glasses, then drizzle each with 1 tbsp Baileys. Top with the sliced bananas, custard and Baileys cream, dividing equally, then drizzle with toffee sauce and finish with grated chocolate. Can be made a few hours ahead.

Notes:

53. Christmas biscuits

• 175g dark muscovado sugar• 85g golden syrup• 100g butter• 3 tsp ground ginger• 1 tsp ground cinnamon• 350g plain flour, plus extra for dusting• 1 tsp bicarbonate of soda• 1 egg, lightly beaten To finish• 100g white chocolate• edible silver balls

Heat the sugar, golden syrup and butter until melted. Mix the spices and flour in a large bowl. Dissolve the bicarbonate of soda in 1 tsp cold water. Make a well in the centre of the dry ingredients, add the melted sugar mix, egg and bicarbonate of soda. Mix well. At this stage the mix will be soft but will firm up on cooling. 2Cover the surface of the biscuit mix with wrapping and leave to cool, then put in the fridge for at least 1 hr to become firm enough to roll out. 3 Heat oven to 190C/170C fan/gas 5. Turn the dough out onto a lightly floured surface and knead briefly. (At this stage the dough can be put into a food bag and kept in the fridge for up to a week.) Cut the dough in half. Thinly roll out one half on a lightly floured surface. Cut into shapes with cutters, such as gifts, trees and hearts, then transfer to baking sheets, leaving a little room for them to spread. If you plan to hang the biscuits up, make a small hole in the top of each one using a skewer. Repeat with remaining dough. 4 Bake for 12-15 mins until they darken slightly. If the holes you have made have closed up, remake them while the biscuits are warm and soft using a skewer. Cool for a few mins on the baking sheets, then transfer to a wire rack to cool and harden up completely. 5 Break up the chocolate and melt in the microwave on Medium for 1-2 mins, or in a small heatproof bowl over simmering water. Drizzle the chocolate over the biscuits, or pipe on shapes or names, then stick a few silver balls into the chocolate. If hung up on the tree, the biscuits will be edible for about a week, but will last a lot longer as decorations.

Notes:

54. Cheese roll-ups

INGREDIENTS (6 Servings)

• 200g self-raising flour , plus extra for dusting• 50g butter , softened• 1 tsp paprika• 100-125ml/3½-4fl oz milk• 50g ready-grated mature cheddar

DIRECTIONS (55 minutes)

1 Heat oven to 220C/200C fan/gas 7. Put the flour and butter in a bowl and rub them together with your fingers. Rubbing in mixture with cold butter is hard and tiring on young fingers, so use slightly softened butter – but not so soft that it is oily. Now stir in the paprika and mix again. Add 100ml milk and mix with a fork until you get a soft dough. Add a splash more milk if the dough is dry. This process will teach you how to feel the dough and decide if it needs more liquid. You can always add more milk if required. 3 On a lightly floured surface, roll out the dough like pastry to about 0.5cm thick. Try to keep a rectangular shape. Only roll in one direction, and roll and turn, roll and turn – by keeping the dough moving, you avoid finding it stuck at the end. 4 Sprinkle the grated cheese on top, then roll up like a sausage along the long side. Cut into 12 thick rings using a table knife. Get an adult to show you how to hold the dough with one hand and cut straight through with the other. 5 Line the baking tray with baking parchment. Place the roll-ups on the parchment, cut-side down, almost touching each other, making sure that you can see the spiral. Get an adult to put them in the oven for you and bake for 20-25 mins until golden and melty. Ask an adult to remove them from the oven, then leave to cool. The cheese roll-ups will keep for up to 3 days in an airtight container.

Notes:

55. Fright Night fancies

• 12 ready-made vanilla cupcakes or fairy cakes , or make your own (see tip)• 2 x 410g cans apricot halves in light syrup, drained (reserve the syrup)• 100g raspberry jam• a little icing sugar or cornflour, for dusting• 500g pack ready-to-roll white fondant icing• black icing pen

1 Remove the cakes from their paper cases – if the tops are rounded, trim them with a serrated knife to make a flat surface. Flip the cakes over and arrange on a large board or cake stand. Brush the cakes all over with the syrup from the drained apricots, then place 1 tsp jam on top of each cake. Put an apricot half on top of the jam, rounded- side facing up. 2 Clean your work surface, then dust with a little icing sugar or cornflour. Roll out the icing to the thickness of a 50p piece – it will be easier if you work with half at a time, keeping the remaining icing well wrapped so it doesn't dry out. Use a 12cm fluted cookie cutter to stamp out 12 circles and, as soon as you cut each one, drape it over a cake. Draw on spooky faces using the black icing pen, then serve. Can be made up to a day ahead; eat leftover cakes within 1 day.

Notes:

56. Courgette muffins

• 50g courgette , cut into chunks• 1 apple , peeled and quartered• 1 orange , halved• 1 egg• 75g butter , melted• 300g self-raising flour• ½ tsp baking powder• ½ tsp cinnamon• 100g golden caster sugar• handful of sultanas• 1 tub soft cheese mixed with 3 tbsp icing sugar, to make icing

1Brush the muffin tin with oil. Ask your grown-up helper to switch the oven to 190C/ 170C fan/gas 5. 2Grate the courgettes and put them in a large bowl. Grate the apple and add to the bowl. Squeeze the orange and add the juice to the bowl. 3Break the egg into a bowl; if any bits of shell get in, scoop them out with a spoon. Stir the butter and egg into the courgette and apple mix. 4Sieve the flour, baking powder and cinnamon into the bowl. Add the sugar and sultanas. 5Mix with a spoon until everything is combined, but don't worry if it is lumpy. 6 Spoon the mixture into the tin. Ask your helper to put it in the oven and cook for 20-25 mins. Cool in the tin, then spread some icing on each.

Notes:

57. Reindeer food

150g porridge oats• 150g jumbo oats• 50g mixed nuts• 25g pumpkin seeds• 25g sunflower seeds• 50g golden caster sugar• 4 tbsp sunflower oil• 2 tbsp maple syrup• ½ tsp ground cinnamon• ½ tsp mixed spice• ½ tsp ground ginger• 100g sultanas• 100g apricots , chopped• mixture of sweets (we used silver balls, chocolate beans, jelly sweets and hundreds and thousands)

DIRECTIONS (55 minutes)

1 Heat oven to 140C/120C fan/gas 1. Put all the ingredients (except the apricots, sultanas and sweets) in a large bowl. Stir everything well, then spread out onto two baking trays in an even layer. Put the tray in the oven for 40 mins. 2 Leave the granola to cool on the tray, then break it up into small chunks and stir in the sultanas and apricots. 3Put the granola in a jar ready for breakfast. To make it suitable for magic reindeer, put a few spoonfuls into a small paper bag and mix in some sweets. 4Tie with string or a ribbon and add a fun label for Father

Notes: